Fives Loaves and Two Fish

Five Loaves and Two Fish

By
Francis Xavier Nguyễn Văn Thuận

Pauline
BOOKS & MEDIA
Boston

Library of Congress Cataloging-in-Publication Data

Nguyen, Francis Xavier Van Thuan, 1928–2002
  [Cinque pani e due pesci. English]
  Five loaves and two fish / by Francis Xavier Nguyen Van Thuan.
    p. cm.
  ISBN 0-8198-2676-6 (pbk.)
  1. Nguyen, Francis Xavier Van Thuan, 1928–2002 2. Christian life—
Catholic authors. I. Title.
  BX2350.3.N4813 2003
  282'.597'09045—dc21

                        2003004575

Cover design by Rosana Usselmann

Cover images: © istockphoto.com/Margarita Lyr;
                © shutterstock.com/ArtMari

"P" and Pauline are registered trademarks of the Daughters of St. Paul.

Translation courtesy of Tinvui Media.

First edition published in Italian under the title *Cinque Pani e Due Pesci*. Copyright © 1997, Edizioni San Paolo, s.r.l., Cinisello Balsamo (MI)

Published by Pauline Books & Media, 50 Saint Pauls Avenue, Boston, MA 02130-3491. www.pauline.org.

Printed in the U.S.A.

Pauline Books & Media is the publishing house of the Daughters of St. Paul, an international congregation of women religious serving the Church with the communications media.

5 6 7 8 9 10   23 22 21 20 19

Contents

Foreword

As a life-long friend and biographer of Cardinal Francis Xavier Nguyen Van Thuan (*The Miracle of Hope*)—and of his mother, Elizabeth Ngo Dinh thi Hiep (*A Lifetime in the Eye of the Storm*)—I have often been asked: "What should I read to really be able to understand Cardinal Van Thuan?" My suggestion has always been to read his books: *The Road of Hope*, *Five Loaves and Two Fish*, and *Testimony of Hope*.

The Road of Hope, written in 1975 while the then Archbishop Thuan was kept in forced residence in Cây Vông Parish, is actually a roadmap from despair to hope. It is a song of defiance in the face of total disaster. The 1,001 simple and profound paragraphs aim at helping those who, like himself at the time, try to find in the most desperate situations a means of sanctification. Every day the archbishop smuggled out a sheet of his "thoughts," which courageous children recopied and delivered to various communities. When the book was completed, Thuan's thoughts, typed and bound, were smuggled out of the country, and soon translated into a dozen languages. The influence of *The Road of Hope* on Christians and non-Christians alike has been unbelievable.

Testimony of Hope, written in January 2000 and published in June of that same year, marked a historical event: an archbishop from Vietnam was asked by the Pope to preach for him and the Roman Curia the yearly spiritual exercises. *Testimony of Hope* reveals some of the archbishop's vision for a strengthened, purified, and revolutionized Church. The Holy Father described the series of sermons as "the breath of divine inspiration." John Paul II added: "He has guided us in deepening our vocation of witnessing the evangelical hope at the beginning of the Third Millennium ... reinforcing in us the consoling certainty that when everything crumbles around us, and perhaps even within us, Christ remains our unfailing support."

Finally, *Five Loaves and Two Fish*, Cardinal Thuan's humble *Magnificat*, extols the marvels that God had accomplished within him. Aware that some people might frown on his attempt to write of his experiences, Cardinal Thuan wanted this small book to make clear that the great wonders in his life were not his doing, but God's alone. Yet, even in 1997, before he began the work, he still feared he might be motivated by pride, though anyone who had the privilege to know him would recognize such was not the case.

The genesis of the book goes back to 1976, when the future cardinal was in solitary confinement at the Phu Khanh Prison, left to rot in a damp, filthy cell without windows. Driven almost to despair, he was inspired by two powerful concepts that were to help him survive thirteen years of imprisonment and make him one of the great spiritual teachers of modern times. First, he understood that he had to choose God over God's works, and second, he had to offer all he had to God and let God turn his offering into abundant nourishment for others, like the little boy in the Gospel, whose five loaves and two fish fed a crowd of over five thousand.

Soon after his release from prison, at our first re-union in Rome in 1989, Thuan was casually recounting to me his thirteen-year experience as a prisoner, when he lowered his voice and began describing the torments and humiliations he suffered at the Phu Khanh Prison Camp. He looked into my eyes and, shaken by sudden emotion, said, "My morale was at its lowest. I was almost in despair. In the darkness of my cell, cut off from my diocese, from God's people, from any human contact, I could not do a thing for anyone; I could not even talk to anyone. I felt completely useless. I prayed, but God did not seem to hear. Then all of a sudden I saw, as if in a vision, Christ on the Cross, crucified and dying. He was completely helpless... certainly worse off than me in my prison cell. Then I heard a voice—was it his voice?—saying: 'At this precise moment on the Cross, I redeemed all the sins of the world.'"

The man who sat in that dark cell understood God's message. He gave his all to the Lord, and the Lord turned the littleness of what he offered into a new fountain of hope for many people around the world.

Later the Cardinal, always on the road giving talks to small and large communities in Europe, America, Africa, and Asia, further developed his original concepts into what would form the core of *Five Loaves and Two Fish*. His talks attracted many people, the young in particular, and he became more and more aware that the book, which had existed within him since 1976, had to be written down.

Somehow, whenever I reread *Five Loaves and Two Fish*, I am always reminded of a drawing the Cardinal sent to his sisters, and of his yearly Christmas message. Cardinal Thuan once drew a cross and placed inscriptions at the top, at the place where Christ rested his head, and where his hands and feet were nailed, which read: "I am nothing," "I am worth nothing," "I deserve nothing," "I can do nothing," and "I know nothing." The Cardinal was not in anguish over his "worthlessness," however. Rather, the words were meant to praise the power of Christ crucified to raise a person out of ignorance, helplessness, and worthlessness, and lift the person up to his presence and into the joy and glory of the Risen Lord.

And at Christmas time, Cardinal Thuan sent cards with this message: "We receive the world as a gift, we accept the world as a mission, and we breathe in the world as we breathe in hope."

Indeed, the Cardinal's personal *Magnificat, Five Loaves and Two Fish,* reflects a great humility, a great joy, and the theological virtue of hope. It calls each of us to give to God the little we have with great confidence that he will turn our small gifts into wonders.

ANDRE N. VAN CHAU

Introduction

Dear young people,

Contemplating a beautiful panorama of green hills and a blue sea with white waves makes me think of Jesus in the midst of the hungry crowd. Looking at you, face to face with the eyes of Jesus, I say to you with all my heart: "Young men and women, I love you!"

In speaking to you today I wish to take as my inspiration a passage from chapter six of Saint John's Gospel. Stand up and listen to the word of Jesus.

> When he looked up and saw a crowd coming toward him, Jesus said to Philip, "Where are we to buy bread for these people to eat?" He said this to test him, for he himself knew exactly what he was going to do. Philip answered him, "Six months' wages would not buy enough for each of them to get a little." One of his disciples, Andrew, Simon

Peter's brother, said to him, "There is a boy here who has five barley loaves and two fish. But what are they among so many people?" Jesus said, "Make the people sit down." Now there was a great deal of grass in the place, so they sat down, about five thousand in all. Then Jesus took the loaves, and when he had given thanks, he distributed them to those who were seated; so also the fish, as much as they wanted. (Jn 6:5–11)

En route to the Jubilee of the year 2000, are we seeking to discover who Jesus is, why we love him, how to let ourselves be loved by him until we come to follow him in the radical nature of our choices, with no thought for the length of the road, the fatigue of the march under the summer sun, and the absence of every comfort.

The Holy Father writes:

In communion with all the people of God who are en route to the Great Jubilee of the year 2000, I would like to invite you this year to fix your gaze on Jesus, Teacher and Lord of our lives, meditating on the words recorded in Saint John's Gospel: "Teacher, where do you live?" "Come and see." (Jn 1:38–39).

(Message for the Twelfth World Youth Day, 1997)

As a young man, a priest, and a bishop, I have already traveled a part of that road, at times with joy, at times with suffering and in prison, but always bearing in my heart an overflowing hope.

I felt a bit uncomfortable when I was asked to speak about my personal experience of following Jesus; it is not a pleasant thing to speak about oneself, but I remember that in the book, *Les Imprevus de Dieu*, the author, the late Cardinal Leon Joseph Suenens, asks Veronica O'Brien: "You have allowed me to speak of your life only today; why did you not allow me to before?" And she responds, "Because now I understand that my life does not belong to me; it is all God's. God can do with it what he will for the good of souls."

John Paul II summarizes this thought well in the title of his autobiography, *Gift and Mystery*, just as Mary did in her *Magnificat*.

Now then, my dear young people, I am going to follow the example in the passage of John's Gospel where Jesus offers five loaves and two fish. These are nothing before a crowd of thousands, but they are all his, and Jesus does everything; it is gift and mystery. Like the boy in the Gospel passage, I will recall my experience in seven points: my five loaves and two fish. These are nothing, but it is all I have. Jesus will do the rest.

Many times I have suffered interiorly because the media wants to hear me tell sensationalistic stories, to accuse, to denounce, to incite opposition, revenge. . . . This is not my goal. My greatest desire is to transmit a message of love, in serenity and truth, in forgiveness and reconciliation. I want to share with you my experiences: how I found Jesus in every moment of my daily life, in discerning between God and the works of God, in prayer, in the Eucharist, in my brothers and sisters, in the Blessed Virgin Mary, who was my guide along the way. Together with you I want to cry out: "Let us live the testament of Jesus! Let us cross the threshold of hope."

Rome,
February 2, 1997
Feast of Mary's Purification

THE FIRST LOAF

Living the Present Moment

It is along the paths of daily life that you can meet
the Lord! ... This is the fundamental dimension of
the encounter: we are not dealing with something,
but with Someone, with the "Living One."

(John Paul II, Message for the
Twelfth World Youth Day, 1997, no. 2)

ﮑﺯﺧﮑﺯﺧ

My name is Francis Xavier Nguyễn Văn Thuận
and I am Vietnamese, but the young people in
Tanzania and Nigeria call me Uncle Francis, which is
a bit simpler, or even better, just Francis.

For eight years I was bishop of Nha Trang, in Central Vietnam, the first diocese entrusted to me. I was happy there, and I always felt a certain predilection for that diocese. On April 23, 1975, Pope Paul VI named me coadjutor archbishop of Saigon. When the Communists arrived in Saigon, they told me that my nomination as coadjutor was a conspiracy of the Vatican and the imperialists to organize a resistance to the Communist regime. About three months later I was called to appear at the Presidential residence where I was arrested. It was the day of the feast of the Blessed Virgin Mary's Assumption: August 15, 1975.

That night, as the police drove me along the 450 kilometer road that brought me to my place of forced residence, many confused thoughts came to my mind: sadness, abandonment, exhaustion after the tension of the three previous months. . . . But one thought broke through clear and bright to disperse all the darkness, the words of Monsignor John Walsh, a missionary bishop in China who said when he was freed after many years of imprisonment: "I am not going to wait. I will live each present moment, filling it to the brim with love."

It was not surprising that this inspiration should come to me, since I had already fostered this conviction throughout my life: *If I spend my time waiting, perhaps the things I look forward to will never happen. The only thing certain to come is death.*

I was forced to live under house arrest in the village of Cây Vông, under the open and secret surveillance of the Communist police, who "mixed in" with the villagers. Day and night I found myself obsessed with the thought: *My people! My people whom I love so dearly: flock without a shepherd! How can I reach my people, at the very moment when they most need their pastor? The Catholic libraries have been confiscated, schools closed, the men and women religious who taught in the schools forced to work in rice fields.* The separation from my people was a shock that devastated my heart. Then I thought: *I will not wait. I will live the present moment, filling it to the brim with love—but how?*

One night, a light came to me: *Francis, it is very simple. Do what Saint Paul did while he was in prison: write letters to the different communities.* The next morning, in October 1975, while it was still dark, I signaled to a seven-year-old boy named Quang, who was returning from 5:00 AM Mass. "Ask your mother to please find some old calendars that I can use for paper." Late that same evening, once again when it was dark, Quang brought me the calendars. Every night during the months of October and November of 1975, I wrote messages for my people from captivity. Every morning,

Quang would come to pick up the pages that I had written and carried them home. There his brothers and sisters would copy down the messages for the various communities. That is how the book *The Road of Hope* came to be written. It was eventually published in eight languages: Vietnamese, English, French, Italian, German, Spanish, Korean, and Chinese.

God's grace gave me the energy to work and to go on even in the most desperate moments. I wrote my messages at night in the space of one-and-a-half months, because I was afraid that I might not be able to finish before I was taken elsewhere. When I got to number 1,001 I decided to stop—so the thoughts are like *A Thousand and One Nights*.

In 1980, when I was in forced residence in Giang Xa, North Vietnam, I wrote (once again, at night and in secret) my second book: *The Road of Hope in Light of God's Word and of Vatican Council II*; and then my third book: *Pilgrims on the Road of Hope*.

I will not wait. I will live the present moment, filling it to the brim with love.

In the Gospel, the apostles wanted to take the easy road: "Lord, send the people away and they can find food. . . ." But Jesus wants to act in the present moment: "Give them something to eat yourselves" (Lk

9:13). On the Cross, when the thief said to him, "Jesus, remember me when you come into your kingdom," he answered, "Today you will be with me in Paradise" (Lk 23:42–43). In the word "today" we hear all of Jesus' forgiveness and love.

Saint Maximilian Kolbe lived and taught this radicalism when he repeated to his novices: "Everything, absolutely, with no conditions." I once heard Dom Helder Camara say: "Life is learning to love." And Mother Teresa of Calcutta wrote to me: "The important thing is not how many actions we perform, but the intensity of love that we put into each action."

How does one reach this intensity of love in the present moment? I simply recall that I must live each day, each moment as if it were the last one of my life. I leave aside everything accidental and concentrate only on the essential; then each word, each gesture, each telephone call, and each decision I make is the most beautiful of my life. I give my love to everyone, my smile to everyone; I am afraid of wasting even one second by living it without meaning. . . .

In *The Road of Hope* I wrote:

Only one moment exists for you in all its beauty and that is the present moment (cf. Mt 6:34; Jas 4:13–15). Live it completely in the love of God. If your life is built up like a large crystal from millions of such moments, it will be a wonderfully beautiful life. Can't you see how easy it could be? (no. 997)

My dear young people, Jesus needs you in the present moment. John Paul II is calling you, insistently, to take up the challenge of today's world:

We are living in an era of great changes: the rapid decline of ideologies that seemed to promise a long resistance to the wear and tear of time; the tracing out on the planet of new confines and frontiers. Humanity often finds itself uncertain, bewildered, and anxious (cf. Mt 9:36). But the word of God knows no decline; throughout history and among changing events, it remains firm and gives light (cf. Mt 24:35). The faith of the Church is founded on Jesus Christ, the one Savior of the world, yesterday and today and for ever (cf. Heb 13:8).

(Message for the Twelfth World Youth Day, 1997, no. 2)

In Prison, for Christ

Jesus, yesterday afternoon,
on the Feast of Mary's Assumption,
I was arrested.
Taken during the night from Saigon
    to Nha Trang,
450 kilometers away,
sitting in a car between two policemen,
I began the experience of a prisoner's life.
There are so many confused feelings in my head:
sadness, fear, tension,
my heart is torn to pieces for having been taken
    away from my people.
I feel humiliated, and I remember the words
    of Sacred Scripture:
"And he was counted among the lawless
—*et cum iniquis deputatus est*" (Lk 22:37).
In the car I passed through three dioceses:
Saigon, Phan Thiet, Nha Trang,
feeling such love for my faithful,
but none of them even knew that their pastor
    was passing by
on the first stop of his *Via Crucis*.
But in this sea of extreme bitterness

I feel freer than ever before.
I have nothing with me, not even a penny,
nothing but my rosary and the companionship
    of Jesus and Mary.
Along the road of captivity I prayed:
"You are my God and my all."
Jesus, now I can say with Saint Paul:
I, Francis, am now a prisoner for the cause
    of Christ
—*ego Franciscus, vinctus Jesus Christi pro vobis*
    (cf. Eph 3:1).
In the darkness of this night,
in the midst of this ocean of anxiety,
    of nightmares,
I slowly wake up again:
"I must confront reality: I am in prison.
If I wait for an opportune moment
to do something truly great,
how many times will such occasions actually
    present themselves?
No, I will seize the occasions that present
    themselves every day.
I must accomplish ordinary actions in an
    extraordinary way."
Jesus, I will not wait,
I will live the present moment,

filling it to the brim with love.

A straight line is made of millions of tiny points
one united to another.

My life, too, is made of millions of seconds
united to each other.

If I arrange every single point perfectly
the line will be straight.

If I live every minute perfectly
my life will be holy.

The road of hope is paved with small steps
of hope.

The life of hope is made of brief moments
of hope.

As you, Jesus, always did what pleased your
Father,

every minute I want to say:

Jesus, I love you,

and my life is always "a new and eternal covenant"
with you.

Every minute I want to sing with your Church:

Glory be to the Father, and to the Son,
and to the Holy Spirit.

> *House arrest in forced residence*
> *Cây Vông (Nha Trang, Central Vietnam)*
> *August 16, 1975, The day after the feast*
> *of Mary's Assumption*

THE SECOND LOAF

Discerning Between God and God's Works

It is true: Jesus is a demanding friend. He points to lofty goals. . . . Break down the barriers of superficiality and fear! Recognize that you are "new" men and women. . . .

(John Paul II, Message for the Twelfth World Youth Day, 1997, no. 3)

CRISTIER

When I was a student in Rome, someone told me: "Your greatest quality is being 'dynamic'; your greatest defect is being 'aggressive.'" In any case, I was very active. I was a scout and a chaplain for a youth group.... There was something that pushed me forward every day: to run against the clock, as it were, because I had to do everything possible to strengthen and build up the Church in my diocese of Nha Trang before the hard times came under Communist rule!

So I worked to increase the number of major seminarians from 42 to 147 in eight years; of minor seminarians from 200 to 500 in four seminaries. I worked for the ongoing formation of priests in six dioceses of the metropolitan Church of Hue; I developed and intensified the formation of new youth movements, lay movements, and of pastoral councils.... I greatly loved my first diocese of Nha Trang.

And then, after eight years, I had to leave everything and go immediately to Saigon, according to the direction of Pope Paul VI. I had no opportunity to say goodbye to all those who were united with me in the same ideal, the same determination, the same sharing of trials as well as joys.

That night, when I recorded my final greeting to the diocese, it was the first time in eight years that I cried, and I cried bitterly!

Then there came my tribulations in Saigon and my arrest. I was taken back to my first diocese in Nha Trang, and placed in the harshest form of captivity—near my former residence. Morning and evening, in the darkness of my cell, I could hear the bells of the Cathedral ringing, and it tore at my heart. At night I could hear the waves of the sea from my cell.

Then I was moved again, traveling in the hold of a ship with 1,500 prisoners. I was taken to the re-education camp of Vinh Quang, in the mountains, and lived amidst other sad and ailing prisoners.

Above all, I suffered the long tribulation of nine years in solitary confinement: seeing only two guards every day, enduring mental torture, absolute emptiness, with no work to do, having to walk back and forth in my cramped cell from morning to night so that I would not become crippled by arthritis. I was on the brink of insanity.

Many times I was tempted, tormented by the fact that I was forty-eight years old, in the prime of my life; I had worked as bishop for eight years, I had acquired a great deal of pastoral experience, and there I was: isolated, inactive, and separated from my people by 1,700 kilometers!

One night I heard a voice encouraging me from the depths of my heart: "Why do you torment yourself so? You must learn to distinguish between God and the works of God. Everything you have done and desire to continue doing: the formation of seminarians, men and women religious, laity, and youth, pastoral visits, constructing schools, foyers for students, missions for the evangelization of non-Christians ... all of these are excellent works, they are God's works, but they are not God! If God wants you to leave all of these works, place them in God's hands immediately and have confidence in him. God will accomplish things infinitely better than you. He will entrust his works to others who are much more capable than you. You have chosen God alone, not his works!"

I had always tried to do God's will, but this light brought me a new strength that completely changed my way of thinking and helped me to overcome moments that were almost physically impossible to overcome.

At times, well-developed programs must be left incomplete, activities begun with great enthusiasm are stalled; large missions are reduced to minor activities. I might become upset and discouraged, but I must ask myself: has the Lord called me to follow him, or to follow this project or that person? Let the Lord work. He will make everything turn out for the best.

When I found myself in the prison at Phù Khánh, confined to a cell without windows, in extremely hot weather, suffocating, I felt myself gradually becoming more lifeless, until I lost consciousness. At times the light in the cell was left on day and night, at other times it was always dark. It was so humid that mushrooms began to grow on my sleeping mat. In the darkness I saw light coming in through a crack at the bottom of the door (to let water run out). So I spent one hundred days on the floor, putting my nose near the crack in order to breath. When it rained and the water level rose; little insects—spiders, millipedes, mosquitoes, etc.—came in and I had no strength left to drive them away.

To choose God and not God's works: God wants me here and nowhere else.

When the Communists threw me into the hold of the ship, *Hai Phong,* with another 1,500 starving and desperate prisoners to be transported north, I saw the desperation, hatred, and the desire for revenge on the faces of my fellow prisoners. I shared their suffering, but immediately the voice called out to me again: "Choose God and not the works of God," and I thought: *In truth, Lord, here is my cathedral and here are the people of God you have given me to take care of. I have to be a confirmation of God's presence in the midst of these desperate, miserable men. It is your will, so I choose it.*

When I arrived at the re-education camp in the mountains of Vinh Phu with 250 prisoners, the majority of whom were not Catholic, the voice called out to me again: "Choose God and not the works of God." I thought: *Yes, Lord, you are sending me here to be your love among my brothers, in the midst of hunger, cold, exhausting labor, humiliation, injustice. I choose you, your will; I am your missionary here.*

From that moment on a new peace flooded my heart that remained with me for thirteen years. I felt my human weakness, but I renewed my choice in the face of difficult situations and I never lacked peace.

When I declare: "For God and for the Church," I remain silent in the presence of God and I ask honestly: "Lord, am I working for you alone? Are you always the essential motive for all I do? I would be ashamed to admit that there are other stronger motives."

Choose God and not God's works. It is a beautiful choice, but a difficult one. John Paul II addresses you:

> Dear young people, like the first disciples, follow Jesus! Do not be afraid to draw near to him. . . . Do not be afraid of the "new life" he is offering. He himself makes it possible for you to receive that life and practice it, with the help of his grace and the gift of his Spirit.
>
> *(Message for the Twelfth World Youth Day, 1997, no. 3)*

John Paul II encourages you with the example of Saint Thérèse of the Child Jesus:

> Walk with her [Thérèse] the humble and simple way of Christian maturity at the school of the

Gospel. Stay with her in the "heart" of the Church, living radically the option for Christ.

(Message for World Youth Day, 1997, no. 9)

This is the choice the young boy in the Gospel made, confidently placing everything he had—five loaves and two fish—into Jesus' hands. Jesus accomplished "God's works," feeding 5,000 men, plus women and children.

GOD AND GOD'S WORKS

Because of your infinite love, Lord,
you called me to follow you,
to be your child and your disciple.

Then you entrusted me with a unique mission:
to be your apostle and witness.
Even so, experience has taught me
that I continue to confuse two realities:
God and the works of God.

God has given me the responsibility
to carry out certain works—
some quite sublime, others more modest,
some noble, others more ordinary.
And so, with a commitment to pastoral work
in parishes and with young people in schools,
with artists and laborers,
in the world of the press, radio, and television,
I gave my entire energy to everything
and poured out all my abilities.
I did not spare anything,
not even my life.

But, while I was so passionately
immersed in action,
I met the defeat of ingratitude,

the refusal to collaborate,
the incomprehension of friends,
the lack of support from leaders,
illness and infirmity,
insufficient resources…

And then when I happened to enjoy success,
when I was the object of everyone's approval,
praise, and affection,
I was suddenly transferred to another position.
So there I was, dazed,
groping about as if in the dark of night:

Why, Lord, are you abandoning me?
I do not want to desert your work,
I want to complete it.
I must finish building the Church…
Why do others attack your work?
Why do they withdraw their support?

Kneeling before your altar
close to the Eucharist,
I heard your answer, Lord:

> *"It is me you are supposed to be following,*
> *not my work!*
> *If I will it, you will finish the work entrusted*
> *to you.*

It matters little who takes over your work
    after you;
that is my business.
Your business is to choose me!"

Solitary confinement, Hanoi (North Vietnam)
February 1985, Memorial of Our Lady of Lourdes

THE THIRD LOAF

Prayer:
A Fixed Point of Reference

"Teacher, where are you staying?" See that you are able to listen again, in the silence of prayer, to Jesus' answer: "Come and see."

(*John Paul II, Message for the Twelfth World Youth Day, 1997*)

❧

After my liberation many people said to me: "Father, in prison you must have had a lot of time to pray." It was not as simple as one might think. The Lord permitted me to experience all my weakness, my physical and mental fragility. Time passes slowly in prison, particularly in solitary confinement. Imagine a week, a month, two months of silence.... They are terribly long, but when they become years, it is an eternity. There is a Vietnamese proverb that says: "One day in prison is like one thousand autumns in freedom." There were days when I was so worn out by exhaustion and illness that I could not manage to say a single prayer! This reminds me of a story.

There was an older man named Jim who would go to church every day at noon for just a few of minutes, and then he would leave. The sacristan was very curious about Jim's daily routine, and one day he stopped him to ask: "Why do you come here every day?"

"I come to pray," Jim answered.

"That's impossible! What prayer can you say in two minutes?"

"I am an old, ignorant man. I pray to God in my own way."

"But what do you say?"

"I say: 'Jesus, here I am, it's Jim.' And then I leave."

After some years, Jim became ill and had to go to the hospital, where he was admitted to the ward for the poor. When it seemed that Jim was dying, a priest and a nurse, a religious sister, stood near his bed.

The priest asked, "Jim, tell us how it is that from the day you came to this ward everything changed for the better? How is it that the patients have become happier, more content, and friendlier?"

"I don't know. When I could walk around, I would try to visit everyone. I greeted them, talked a bit with them. When I couldn't get out of bed I called everyone over to me to make them laugh, to make them happy. With Jim they are always happy!"

"But why are *you* happy?"

"Well aren't you happy when you receive a visitor?" asked Jim.

"Of course, but we have never seen anyone come to visit you."

"When I came here I asked you for two chairs. One was for you, Father, and one was reserved for my guest."

"But what guest?" the priest asked.

"I used to go to church to visit Jesus every day at noon. But when I couldn't do that anymore, Jesus came here."

"Jesus comes to visit you? What does he say?"

"He says: 'Jim, here I am, it's Jesus!'"

Before dying, Jim smiled and gestured with his hand toward the chair next to his bed, as if inviting someone to sit down. He smiled for the last time and closed his eyes.

When my strength failed and I could not even pray, I repeated: "Jesus, here I am, it's Francis." Joy and consolation would come to me and I experienced Jesus responding: "Francis, here I am, it's Jesus."

If you ask what are your favorite prayers, in all sincerity, I would say I love best the short and simple prayers of the Gospel:

"They have no more wine . . ." (Jn 2:3).

"Magnificat . . ." (Lk 1:46–55).

"Father, forgive them . . ." (Lk 23:34).

"Into your hands . . ." (Lk 23:46).

"That they may be one . . ." (Jn 17:21).

"Be merciful to me a sinner . . ." (Lk 18:13).

"Remember me when you come into your kingdom" (Lk 23:42).

I also love to pray with the whole of God's word, with the liturgical prayers, the psalms, the canticles. I greatly love Gregorian chant, which in large part I recall from memory. Thanks to my seminary formation, these liturgical songs entered deep into my heart! Then there are the prayers of my native language, so moving, that my whole family prayed together every evening in our chapel, which reminds me of my childhood. Above all, there are the three Hail Marys and the *Memorare* that my mother taught me to recite morning and evening.

As I said, I spent nine years in solitary confinement, having contact with only two guards. To avoid illnesses like arthritis, a danger because I was never allowed to leave my cell, I would walk back and forth all day, massage my muscles, do physical exercises, etc., while praying with songs like the *Miserere*, *Te Deum*, *Veni Creator*, and the hymn of the martyrs, *Sanctorum Meritis*. These hymns of the Church, inspired by God's word, provided me with a great deal of courage to follow Jesus. To come to truly value these beautiful prayers it was necessary to experience the obscurity of prison and to become aware that our sufferings can be offered for the Church's fidelity. I sensed this intention, which I directed to Jesus in communion with the Holy Father and the whole Church, in an irresistible way when I repeated throughout the day: "Through him, with him, in him *(per ipsum et cum ipso et in ipso)*. . . ."

The simple prayer of a Communist (yes, a Communist!) comes to my mind. At first this man was sent to spy on me, but later he became my friend. Before his liberation he said: "My house is three kilometers from the shrine of the Madonna of La Vang. I promise to go there to pray for you." I believed in his friendship, but I certainly doubted that a Communist would pray to the Madonna. Then one day, perhaps six years later, while I was in solitary confinement, I received a letter from him! He wrote: "Dear friend, I promised you that I would go to pray for you at the shrine of Our Lady of

La Vang. I do so every Sunday, if it isn't raining. When I hear the church bells ringing, I ride my bicycle there. I pray for you like this: 'Madonna, I am not a Christian; I do not know how to pray; but I ask you to give Mr. Thuan what he desires.'" I was moved to the very depths of my heart, and thought that the Madonna would certainly answer him.

In the Gospel passage on which we are meditating, we see that Jesus prayed before performing the miracle of the multiplication of the loaves and fish to feed the hungry people. Jesus wants to teach us that it is necessary to pray before pastoral, social, and charitable works.

John Paul II says to you:

> Talk with Jesus in prayer and while listening to the word; experience the joy of reconciliation in the sacrament of Penance; receive the Body and Blood of Christ in the Eucharist. . . . You will discover the truth about yourselves and your inner unity, and you will find a "Thou" who gives the cure for anxieties, for nightmares, and for the unbridled subjectivism that leaves you no peace.

> *(Message for the Twelfth World Youth Day 1997, no. 3)*

Brief Gospel Prayers

Lord, you have given me a model for prayer,
in fact, you left only one: the *Our Father*.
It is brief, concise, and packed with meaning.
Your life, Lord, is a sincere and simple prayer
addressed to your Father.
Your prayer was sometimes long,
like your ardent and spontaneous priestly prayer
after the Last Supper.

But more often your prayers
and those of your mother and your apostles
were brief, but beautiful,
linking together the actions of daily life.
I, who often feel weak and indifferent,
love to recall those brief prayers as I kneel before
    the Eucharist,
sit at my desk, or walk along a street alone.
The more I repeat them,
the more they penetrate me.
I am close to you, Lord.

> *Father, forgive them, for they know not what
>   they do (Lk 23:34).*

> *Father, that they may be one (Jn 17:22).*

> *I am the handmaid of the Lord (Lk 1:38).*

They have no wine (Jn 2:3).

Behold your son, behold your Mother!
        (Jn 19:26–27)

Remember me when you come into your
        kingdom (Lk 23:42).

Lord, what do you want me to do? (Acts 22:10)

Lord, you know all things; you know that
        I love you (Jn 21:17).

Lord, have mercy on me, a poor sinner
        (Lk 18:39).

My God, my God, why have you abandoned me?
        (Mk 15:34)

All of these brief prayers,
linked one to another,
form a life of prayer.
Like a chain of discreet gestures, glances,
        and intimate words,
they form a life of love.
They keep us in an atmosphere of prayer
without distracting us from our present tasks,
but helping us to live our day more conscious
        of God.

                    Solitary confinement, Hanoi (North Vietnam)
                    March 25, 1987, Feast of the Annunciation

The Eucharist:
My Only Strength

Around the Eucharistic table the harmonious unity
of the Church is realized and made manifest; the
mystery of missionary communion, in which all feel
that they are children, sisters and brothers.

(John Paul II, Message for the Twelfth
World Youth Day, 1997, no. 7)

❧❦❧

"Were you able to celebrate the Eucharist
in prison?" is one question that many people
have asked me. And they are right to ask: The Eucharist
is the most beautiful prayer; it is the culmination of

the life of Jesus. When I answer "yes," I already know the next question: "How were you able to obtain the bread and wine?"

When I was arrested, I had to leave immediately, with empty hands. The next day I was allowed to request in writing the things I needed most: clothes, toothpaste. . . . I wrote to my addressee: "Please, could you send me a bit of medicine for my bad stomach?" The faithful understood what I meant and they sent a little bottle of wine for Mass, which they labeled "stomach medicine," as well as some hosts sealed in a flashlight to protect them from the humidity. The police asked me: "Do you have a bad stomach?"

"Yes," I answered.

"Here's some medicine for you."

I will never be able to express my immense joy: every day, with three drops of wine and one drop of water in the palm of my hand, I celebrated my Mass.

It depended on the situation, however. On the boat that brought us north, I celebrated at night with the prisoners who received Communion around me. At times I had to celebrate while everyone was bathing after calisthenics. In the re-education camp, the prisoners were divided into groups of fifty; we slept on common beds and everyone had the right to fifty centimeters of space. We arranged it so that there were five

Catholics near me. At 9:30 PM the lights were turned off and everyone had to sleep. I curled up on the bed to celebrate Mass, from memory, and I distributed Communion by reaching under the mosquito netting covering us. We made small containers from cigarette packages in which to reserve the Blessed Sacrament. Jesus in the Eucharist was always with me in my shirt pocket.

In *The Road of Hope* I wrote: "You believe in one strength: the Eucharist, the Lord's Body and Blood that gives you life.'I have come so that they may have life and have it abundantly' (Jn 10:10). As manna nourished the Israelites on their journey to the Promised Land, so the Eucharist nourishes you on your road of hope" (no. 983).

We had weekly indoctrination sessions in which the whole camp had to participate. During our break, I and my Catholic companions took advantage of the opportunity to pass to each, or to the other four groups of prisoners, the little container that held the Blessed Sacrament: they all knew that Jesus was among them, he who could heal all their physical and mental suffering. At night, the prisoners took turns for adoration; Jesus helped us in a tremendous way with his silent presence. Many Christians regained the fervor of their faith during those days, and Buddhists and other non-Christians converted. The strength of Jesus' love is irresistible. The darkness of prison became light; the seed germinated underground during the storm.

Every time I offer Mass I have the opportunity to extend my hands and nail myself to the Cross with Jesus, to drink with him the bitter cup.

Every day, praying and hearing the words of the consecration, I confirm with all my heart and with all my soul a new covenant, an eternal covenant between me and Jesus, through his Blood mixed with mine (cf. 1 Cor 11:23–25).

Jesus began a revolution from the Cross. Your revolution must begin from the Eucharistic table and has to be carried forward from there. In this way you will be able to renew humanity.

In my nine years in solitary confinement, I celebrated Mass every day around 3:00 PM: the hour of Jesus' agony and death on the Cross. I was alone, so I could sing the Mass as I wished: in Latin, French, or Vietnamese. . . . I always carried the little container holding the Blessed Sacrament: "You in me and I in you" (Jn 6:20). These were the most beautiful Masses of my life.

At 9:00 PM I made an hour of adoration, singing over the noise of the loudspeakers that blared from 5:00 AM to 11:30 PM every day the *Lauda Sion, Pange*

Lingua, Adoro Te, Te Deum, and other hymns in Vietnamese. I felt a singular peace of spirit and of heart, and the joy and serenity of the companionship of Jesus, Mary, and Saint Joseph. I sang the *Salve Regina, Salve Mater, Alma Redemptoris Mater, Regina Coeli* . . . in union with the Universal Church. Despite the accusations and the calumnies leveled against the Church by my interrogators, I sang *Tu es Petrus, Oremus Pro, Pontifice Nostro, Christus Vincit.* . . . Just as Jesus relieved the hunger of the crowd that followed him in the desert, it is he himself who continues to be the food of eternal life in the Eucharist.

In the Eucharist we announce the death of Jesus and we proclaim his resurrection. There were moments of infinite sadness; how did I survive? By looking at Jesus crucified and abandoned on the Cross. To human eyes the life of Jesus was a defeat, a disappointment, a failure. However, in God's eyes Jesus accomplished the most important act of his life on the Cross, because he poured out his blood to save the world. How greatly Jesus was united to God when on the Cross he could no longer preach, cure the sick, visit the towns and villages, perform miracles, but remained absolutely immobile!

Jesus is my first example of radical love for the Father and for souls. Jesus gave everything: "He loved them to the end—*in finem dilexit*" (Jn 13:1), up to the very moment of the"It is finished—*consummatum est*" (Jn 19:30).

And the Father loved the world: "For God so loved the world that he gave his only Son—*ut Filium suum unigenitum traderet*" (Jn 3:16). To give himself as bread "for the life of the world—*pro mundi vita*" (Jn 6:51).

Jesus said: "I have compassion for the crowd—*Misereor super turbam*" (Mt 15:32). The multiplication of the loaves is an announcement, a sign of the Eucharist that Jesus will soon institute.

My dear young people listen to the Holy Father:

> Jesus lives among us in the Eucharist. . . . Amidst the uncertainties and distractions of daily life, imitate the disciples on the road to Emmaus. . . . Call out to Jesus to remain with you always along the many roads to Emmaus of our time. May he be your strength, your point of reference, and your enduring hope.

> *(Message for the Twelfth World Youth Day 1997, no. 7)*

THE PRESENT AND THE PAST

Beloved Jesus,
this evening, sitting toward the back of my cell,
without light, without a window, in the stiflingly
     heat,
I think with overwhelming nostalgia of my
     pastoral life.

Eight years as bishop
living in the residence only two kilometers
     from my prison cell,
on the same street, near the same sea shore . . .
I can hear the waves of the Pacific
and the bells of the cathedral.

Once I used to celebrate the Eucharist
     with a gold-plated paten and chalice;
now I hold your Blood in the palm of my hand.

Once I used to travel the world over to attend
     conferences and meetings;
*now I am confined to a narrow cell without
     a window.*

Once I used to visit you in the tabernacle;
now I carry you, night and day, in my shirt pocket.

Once I used to celebrate Mass for thousands
    of faithful;
*now, in the darkness of the night, I give Communion
    under a mosquito net.*

Once I used to preach the spiritual exercises to
priests, religious, lay people . . .
*now a priest, who is also a prisoner,
    preaches the exercises of Saint Ignatius to me
    through a crack in the wall.*

Once I used to have solemn benediction of the
    Blessed Sacrament in the cathedral;
*now I have Eucharistic adoration in silence every
    night at 9:00, softly singing the* Tantum Ergo
    and the Salve Regina, *and concluding with this
    short prayer: "Lord, now I am content to accept
    everything from your hands:
    all the sadness, the suffering, the anguish,
    even my death. Amen."*

I am happy, here in this cell,
where white mushrooms are growing on my
    sleeping mat,
because you are with me,
because you want me to live here with you.

I have spoken much in my lifetime;
now I speak no more.

It is your turn to speak to me, Jesus.
I am listening to you:
What have you whispered to me?
Is it a dream?
You do not speak to me of the past or of the
     present,
you do not speak of my sufferings or of my
     anguish
you speak to me of your plans, of my mission.

So I sing of your mercy in the darkness,
in my weakness, in my annihilation.
I accept my cross
and I plant it,
with my own two hands,
in my heart.

If you were to permit me to choose
I would change nothing,
because you are with me!
I am no longer afraid,
I have understood.
I am following you in your passion
and in your resurrection.

Solitary confinement,
Phú Khành prison (Central Vietnam)
October 7, 1976, Feast of the Holy Rosary

THE FIFTH LOAF

Love and Unity:
The Testimony of Jesus

Dear young people, you are called to be credible
witnesses to the Gospel of Christ, who makes all
things new But how are you to be recognized as
true disciples of Christ? By the fact that you have
"Love for one another" (Jn 15:35).

*(John Paul II, Message for the Twelfth
World Youth Day, 1997, no. 8)*

꧁꧂

One night when I was very sick in the prison
of Phú Khành, I saw a policeman walk by and
I shouted: "For goodness' sake, I am very sick; please

give me some medicine!" He responded: "There is no goodness here, or love; there is only responsibility." This is the atmosphere we breathed in prison.

When I was put into solitary confinement, I was initially entrusted to a group of five guards, two of whom always accompanied me. The wardens had them changed every two weeks so that they would not become "contaminated" by me. Later they decided not to rotate the guards, or they might all become contaminated!

At first, the guards did not speak to me. They responded to my questions with a "yes" and "no" only. It was truly sad. I wanted to be kind and courteous with them, but it was impossible because they refused my kindness and avoided speaking with me. I had nothing to give them. I was a prisoner; even all of my clothes were stamped with "cai tao," that is, "re-education camp," in big letters. What could I do?

One night a thought came to me: "Francis, you are still very rich. You have the love of Christ in your heart. Love them as Jesus has loved you."

The next day I began to love them, to love Jesus in them. I smiled and exchanged kind words. I began to tell them stories of my travels overseas, how people lived in other countries: America, Canada, Japan, the Philippines, Singapore, France, Germany . . . of

their economy, freedom, technology. This stirred their
curiosity and impelled them to ask me about many,
many things. Little by little we became friends. They
wanted to learn foreign languages: French, English,
Latin. . . . So my guards became my students! The
atmosphere in the prison changed greatly, and the
quality of our relationship improved—even up to
the level of the police chiefs. When they witnessed
the sincerity of my relationship with the guards, not
only did they ask me to continue helping them in the
study of foreign languages, but they also sent more
guards to study under me.

One day a police chief asked me, "What do you
think of the newspaper, *The Catholic?*"

"That newspaper does no good to Catholics or the
government. Rather, it has only managed to enlarge the
gulf of separation between the two," I answered.

"Yes, because it expresses itself badly; they misuse
religious terms, and they speak offensively. How can
we remedy this situation?"

"First, you must understand the exact meaning of
the religious terminology used. . . ."

"Could you help us?" he interrupted.

"Yes. I propose writing a dictionary of religious
terms, from A to Z. When you have a moment, I will
explain it to you. I hope that in this way you can better

understand the structure, the activities, the history, and the development of the Church ..."

The police gave me paper on which I wrote out my dictionary of 1,500 terms in French, English, Italian, Latin, Spanish, and Chinese, with the definitions in Vietnamese. Thus, with these definitions, my responses to their questions about the Church, as well as my acceptance of their criticism, this document gradually became a "practical catechism." The police were very curious to learn for example the meaning of patriarch, abbot, the difference between the Orthodox, Catholic, Anglican, and Lutheran churches, and how the Vatican ran its finances, etc.

This systematic dialogue, from A to Z, helped to correct many mistaken ideas, many preconceived notions of the faith. It became more interesting every day, even fascinating.

During that time, I heard that a group of twenty young members of the secret police were studying Latin with a former catechist, in order to be able to understand ecclesiastical documents. One of my guards belonged to the group and one day he asked me if I would teach him a song in Latin.

"There are many Latin hymns, and all so beautiful," I responded.

"Well, you sing them for me and I'll choose one," he said.

So I sang the *Salve Regina, Veni Creator, Ave Maris Stella*. . . . Can you imagine which hymn he chose? The *Veni Creator!*

I cannot say how truly moving it was to hear this young Communist police officer going down the wooden staircase at 7:00 every morning for calisthenics, and then returning to his room to shower while singing the *Veni Creator*—there in the prison.

When there is love, one feels joy and peace, because Jesus is there among us. "Wear only one garment and speak only one language: charity" (*The Road of Hope*, no. 984).

One rainy day in the mountains of Vinh Phu, in the prison of Vinh Quang, I had to chop wood and I said to the guard:

"Can I ask you a favor?"

"What is it? Perhaps I can help you?"

"I would like to take a piece of wood and carve it in the form of a cross."

"Don't you know that religious symbols are seriously prohibited?" he asked in alarm.

"Yes, I know. But we are friends, and I promise to hide it."

"It would be extremely dangerous for both of us" he protested.

"You close your eyes; I will do it now very cautiously."

He left me alone. I cut the cross and kept it hidden in a piece of soap until my liberation. This piece of wood, now with a metal covering, became my pectoral cross.

In another prison I asked my guard—who had already become my friend—for a length of electric wire. He was surprised by my request: "At the police academy we learned that when prisoners want electric wire it means that they are planning to commit suicide."

"Catholic priests do not commit suicide," I explained.

"Then what are you going to do with electric wire?"

"I would like to make a chain so I can wear my cross," I said.

"How can you make a chain with electric wire? That's impossible!"

"If you bring me two little pincers, I will show you how," I persisted.

"No, it's too dangerous!"

"But we are friends," I pleaded.

He hesitated and then said, "I will give you an answer in three days."

After three days he said to me, "It is hard to refuse you anything. I thought that this evening I would let the other guard off duty to go to see the movie, *Hanoi by Night*. I will bring two small pincers so we can work from 7:00 to 11:00—the other guard will have returned by then. But we have to finish before he returns. If he sees us, it will be dangerous for us both."

That night we cut the electric wire into pieces the size of match sticks, and then made the links and joined them . . . and the chain was finished before 11:00.

I wear this cross and this chain daily not because they are reminders to me of prison, but because they represent a profound conviction that is a constant reference point for me: only Christian love—not weapons, not threats, not the media—can change hearts.

It was very difficult for my guards to understand how it is possible for one to forgive, to love one's enemies, to be reconciled with them.

"Do you really love us?" they would ask.

"Yes, I sincerely love you."

Incredulous, they persisted: "Even when we have treated you so badly? When you have suffered in prison for so many years without ever having a trial?"

"Yes, I still love you."

"That's impossible! Perhaps it's not true!"

"Think about the years we have been here together" I insisted. "You have seen for yourselves that it's true. I really love you!"

"When you are freed you won't try to take revenge on us or our families?"

"No, I will continue loving you, even if you want to kill me."

"But why?" they asked.

"Because Jesus has taught me to love you; if I do not, I am no longer worthy of being called a Christian."

There is not enough time to tell you other very moving stories of things that happened, all of them testimonies of the liberating power of the love of Jesus.

In the Gospel, seeing the crowd that has followed him for three days, Jesus said, "I have compassion for the crowd—*Misereor super turbam*" (Mt 15:32), "they are like sheep without a shepherd" (cf. Mk 6:34). . . . At the most dramatic moments of my imprisonment, when I was on the verge of collapse, without enough strength even to pray or meditate I looked for a way to sum up the essence of my prayer, of the message of Jesus. And I used this phrase: *I am living the testimony of Jesus.* That is, loving others as Jesus has loved me, in forgiveness, in mercy, to the point of being one with them as he prayed: "That they may all be one, as you, Father, are in me and I am in you" (Jn 17:21). I prayed so often: *I am living the testament of the love of Jesus.*

I want to be the boy who offered everything he had. It was nothing, five loaves and two fish, but it was "everything" he had, which he gave up to be "an instrument of the love of Jesus."

Dear young people, Pope John Paul II sends out his message to you:

> You will meet Jesus where men and women are suffering and hoping: in the little villages, scattered across the continents and seemingly on the fringe of history, as Nazareth was when God sent his Angel to Mary; in the huge metropolises where millions of human beings live, often as strangers.
>
> Jesus is living next to you. . . . His visage is that of the poorest, of the marginalized, who not infrequently are victims of an unjust model of development in which profit is given first place and the human being is made a means rather than an end. . . .
>
> Jesus dwells among those who call on him without having known him; among those who, after beginning to know him, have lost him through no fault of their own; among those who seek him in sincerity of heart, while coming from different cultural and religious contexts (cf. *Lumen Gentium*, no. 16).
>
> Jesus dwells among the men and women "honored with the name of Christian" (cf. *Lumen*

Gentium, no. 15). On the eve of the third millennium, it is becoming every day a more urgent duty
to repair the scandal of the division among Christians.

*(Message for the Twelfth
World Youth Day 1997, nos. 4, 5)*

The greatest mistake is in not being aware that
others are Christ. There are very many people who will
not discover it until their last day.

Jesus was abandoned on the Cross, and in the same
way he is still abandoned in every brother and sister
who suffers in every corner of the world. Charity has no
boundaries; if it has boundaries, it is no longer charity.

Consecration

Most loving and all-powerful Father,
you are the source of my hope and my joy.

1. *"All that is mine is yours" (Lk 15:31).*
   "Ask and you will receive" (Mt 7:7).

   Father, I firmly believe that your love is infinite.
   How could the love of your children vie
       with yours?
   Oh! The immensity of your fatherly love!
   All that is yours is mine.
   You counseled me to pray with sincerity,
   and I entrust myself to you, Father,
   full of goodness.

2. *"All is grace" (Rom 4:16).*
   "Your Father knows what you need" (Mt 6:8).

   Father, I firmly believe that from the beginning
   you provided everything for my greatest good.
   You never cease guiding my life.
   You accompany each of my steps.
   What could I fear?
   Prostrate before you, I adore your holy will.
   I put myself entirely into your hands,

knowing that all things come about through you.
I am your child; I believe that everything is grace.

3. *"I can do all things through Christ who strengthens
        me" (Phil 4:13).*
    "To the praise of his glory" (Eph 1:6).

    Father, I firmly believe that nothing
    surpasses the omnipotence of your Providence.
    Your love is infinite.
    I want to accept everything with a joyful heart:
    Praise and eternal thanksgiving,
    united to the Virgin Mary, Saint Joseph,
        and the angels.
    I join my voice to those of people of all nations
    to sing the glory of God for ever and ever. Amen.

4. *"Do all for the glory of God" (1 Cor 10:31).*
    "Your will be done" (Mt 6:10).

    Father, I firmly believe without hesitation,
    that you work and act in me.
    I am the object of your affection and tenderness.
    I ask you to realize in me
    all that can bring you greater glory.
    I ask only for your glory,
    that is enough to satisfy me and to make
        me happy;

this is my greatest aspiration,
the most urgent desire of my soul.

5. *"All for the mission! All for the Church!"*

Father, I firmly believe
that you have entrusted me with a mission,
engraved entirely with your love.
You prepare the way for me.
I will not cease readying myself,
and being firm in my resolution.
Yes, I have resolved
to become a silent offering.
I shall serve as an instrument
in the Father's hands.
I will offer my sacrifice,
moment by moment,
through my love for the Church.
"Here I am; I am ready!"

6. *"With fervent desire I have desired to eat this
Passover with you" (Lk 22:15).*
"It is consummated" (Jn 19:30).

My beloved Father!
United to the sacrifice
of the Eucharistic celebration,
which I do not cease to offer,

I kneel at this moment
and speak this word that comes from my heart:
"sacrifice"; a sacrifice that accepts humiliation
    as well as glory,
a joyful and complete sacrifice
that sings of all my hope and all my love.

Solitary Confinement,
Phù Khánh prison (Central Vietnam)
September 1, 1976, Feast of the Vietnamese Martyrs

My First Love:
The Immaculate Virgin Mary

To Mary I entrust . . . the hopes and expectations
of the young people who, with her, repeat in every
corner of the planet: "Behold, I am the handmaid
of the Lord; let it be done to me according to your
word" (Lk 1:38) . . . who are ready then to proclaim
to their contemporaries, as did the apostles: "We
have found the Messiah!" (Jn 1:41)

(John Paul II, Message for the Twelfth
World Youth Day, 1997, no. 10)

❦

"Immaculate Mary, my first love": I read these words
from Saint John Mary Vianney, the Cure of Ars,

57

in a book by Francis Trochu while I was in the minor seminary.

My mother instilled in my heart a love for Mary when I was a child. Every evening, after our family prayers, my grandmother would pray another Rosary. When I asked her why, she said, "I pray this Rosary for priests." She did not know how to read or write, but grandmothers and mothers like her shape vocations in hearts.

You may ask how Mary helped me overcome the numerous trials of my life. I will share with you some episodes, which still remain vivid in my memory.

When I was a priest studying in Rome in September of 1957, I went to the grotto of Lourdes to pray to the Madonna. The words that the Immaculate Virgin Mary spoke to Saint Bernadette seemed to be directed to me as well: "Bernadette, I do not promise you joy and consolation on this earth, but trials and suffering." It was not without fear that I accepted this message. After graduating, I returned to Vietnam to go on to become a seminary professor, the rector of the seminary, the Vicar General, and then, in 1967, the bishop of Nha Trang. One could say, thanks be to God, that my pastoral ministry was crowned with success.

There were other occasions when I returned to pray at the grotto of Lourdes. Each time I wondered if I had not been mistaken: Perhaps the words spoken to Bernadette are not for me after all? My daily crosses are not so unbearable. In any case, I am ready to do whatever God wills.

Then the year 1975 arrived and with it my arrest, imprisonment, years of solitary confinement, and more than thirteen years in captivity. It was then that I understood that the Madonna had been preparing me since 1957!"I do not promise you joy and consolation in this life, but trials and suffering." Every day I understood more intimately the deep meaning of this message, and I confidently abandoned myself into Mary's hands.

When my physical and moral miseries in prison become too heavy and prevented me from praying, then I said the Hail Mary; I repeated the Hail Mary hundreds of times. I placed everything into the hands of the Immaculate Virgin Mary, praying for her to distribute graces to all those in need of them in the Church. Everything with Mary, through Mary, and in Mary.

I did not offer prayers of intercession only, but I often ask: "Mother, what can I do for you? I am ready to fulfill your wishes, to carry out your desires for the kingdom of Jesus." Then immense peace would pervade my heart, I was no longer afraid.

When I prayed to Mary, I never forgot Saint Joseph, her spouse, with his special titles [Mirror of patience,

Lover of poverty, Patron of the dying, Protector of the Holy Church, etc.]—this is a desire of Mary and Jesus, who have a great love for Saint Joseph.

The Immaculate Virgin Mary did not abandon me. She accompanied me the whole way along my march through the darkness of prison. In those days of unspeakable trials, I prayed to Mary with complete simplicity and trust: "Mother, if you see that I can still be useful to your Church, then let me leave prison on one of your feast days!"

One rainy day, while I was preparing my meal, I heard the guards' telephone ringing. "Maybe it's a call for me! After all, today is November 21, the feast of Mary's Presentation in the Temple!"

Five minutes later, a guard came to my cell. "Have you eaten?" he asked.

"Not yet, I am still preparing."

"Well then, after you eat, make yourself presentable. You are going to see the chief."

"What chief?" I asked.

"I don't know. That's what they told me to tell you. Good luck!"

I was driven to a building where I met the Minister of the Interior, that is, of the police. After a few polite words of greeting he asked me, "Do you have any desires to express."

"Yes. I want my freedom."

"When?" he asked.

"Today."

He looked at me with great surprise. I explained: "Your Excellency, I have been in prison for too long—under three pontificates: Paul VI, John Paul I, and John Paul II; and besides that, under *four* Secretary Generals of the Soviet Communist Party: Brezhnev, Andropov, Chernenko, and Gorbachev!"

He began to laugh and nodded his head: "That's true, that's very true!" And turning toward his secretary he said: "Do whatever is necessary to fulfill his request."

Suddenly the wardens had to take care of the necessary formalities for my release, but at that moment I thought: *Today is the feast of Mary's Presentation. It is Mary who is setting me free. Thank you, Mary!*

The moment I feel myself to be most especially Mary's son is during the holy Mass. When I say the words of the consecration I am identified with Jesus, *in persona Christi.*

You may ask what role Mary has in my radical choice for Jesus. On the Cross Jesus said to John: "Behold your mother!" (Jn 19:29) After the institution of the Eucharist, the Lord could not have left me anything greater than his Mother.

For me, Mary is like a living Gospel: portable, widely available, more accessible than the lives of saints.

Mary is my Mother, given to me by Jesus. When a child is afraid, in difficulty, or suffering, his or her first reaction is to cry out: "Mamma, mamma!" This word is everything for a child.

Mary did not worry only about Jesus, but she showed her solicitude also for Elizabeth, for John, and for the couple at Cana.

I love very much the words of Saint Thérèse of Lisieux: "I would so much like to be a priest so that I could speak of Mary to everyone."

At first I used to run to Mary, my Mother who always helped me. Now I listen to Mary, who says to me: "Do whatever he tells you" (Jn 2:5), and I often ask her: "Mother, what can I do for you?" I continue being her child, but a responsible child who knows how to share his Mother's concerns.

Mary's life can be summed up in three words: *Ecce, Fiat, Magnificat.*

Ecce: "Behold the handmaid of the Lord" (Lk 1:38).

Fiat: "May it be done unto me according to your word" (Lk 1:38).

Magnificat: "My soul magnifies the Lord" (Lk 1:46).

MARY, MY MOTHER

Mary, Mother of Jesus, my Mother,
I want to call you *our* Mother,
to feel close to Jesus
and to all my brothers and sisters.
Come live in me, Mary, with Jesus your
    beloved Son,
in silence and in waiting,
in prayer and in offering,
in communion with the Holy Trinity and
    the Church,
in the fervor of your *Magnificat*, that message
    of complete renewal;
in union with Joseph, your most holy spouse;
in your humble and loving work to accomplish
    Jesus' will;
in your love for Jesus, for Joseph,
for the Church, all for all humanity;
in your unshakeable faith in the midst of
    so many trials
endured for the kingdom;
in your ceaselessly active hope
to build a new world of righteousness and peace,
of happiness and true tenderness;

in the perfection of your virtues in the
    Holy Spirit,
so as to become a witness of the Good News,
an apostle of the Gospel.

Continue, O Mother,
to work, to pray, to love, and to sacrifice in me;
continue to carry out the Father's will,
continue to be the Mother of humanity;
continue to live Jesus' passion and resurrection
    in me.
O Mother, I consecrate myself entirely to you,
    now and for ever.
In living your spirit and that of Joseph,
I shall live the spirit of Jesus.
I love you, O our Mother,
with Jesus, Joseph, the angels, the saints,
    and all people.
I will share your labors, your cares, and
    your struggle
for the kingdom of the Lord Jesus. Amen.

Solitary confinement, Hanoi (North Vietnam)
January 1, 1986, Solemnity of Mary, Mother of God

THE SECOND FISH

I Have Chosen Jesus

God is Love; every person is loved by God.... This is a message that you, young people of today, are called to receive and to shout aloud to those of your own age: "Man is loved by God! This very simple yet profound proclamation is owed to humanity by the Church" (*Christifideles Laici*, no. 34).

> (*John Paul II, Message for the Twelfth World Youth Day, 1997, no. 9*)

꧁꧂

I have shared with you some of my experiences following Jesus so as to find him, to live beside him, and thus to carry his message to everyone.

Perhaps you might ask: How can one practice complete union with Jesus in a life tossed about by so many changes? I have not hidden the answer from you, but for clarity I will rewrite it, my secret! (cf. *The Road of Hope*, nos. 979–1001).

At the beginning of the last chapter of *The Road of Hope*, there are twenty-four paragraphs; I wanted them to correspond to the hours in a day. In each of these twenty-four paragraphs, I repeated the word "one": one revolution, one campaign, one message, one strength.... They are very practical points. If we live the twenty-four hours of our day radically for Jesus, we will be saints. They are twenty-four stars that light up our road of hope.

I will not explain these thoughts to you; instead I invite you to meditate on them calmly, as if Jesus were speaking sweetly, intimately to your hearts. Do not be afraid to listen to him, to speak with him. Do not hesitate. Reread these thoughts once a week. You will find that grace will shine forth, transforming your lives.

We will conclude with the prayer "I Have Chosen Jesus"; be sure to note the fourteen steps in the life of Jesus.

1   You want one revolution: to renew the world. You will be able to fulfill this precious and noble mission that God has entrusted to you only with

"the power of the Holy Spirit." Every day, where you live, prepare a new Pentecost.

2　Commit yourself to one campaign, the goal of which is to make everyone happy. Sacrifice yourself continually, with Jesus, so as to bring peace to hearts and souls, and development and prosperity to peoples. This will be your spirituality, dis-creete and concrete at the same time.

3　Stay faithful to the ideal of the apostle: "Give your life for your brothers and sisters." In fact, "No one has greater love than this" (Jn 15:13). Spend all your energies without rest, and be ready to give yourself to "conquer" your neighbor for God.

4　Shout one message: "All one," that is, unity among Catholics, unity among Christians, and unity among nations. "As the Father and the Son are one" (cf. Jn 17:22–23).

5　Believe in one strength: the Eucharist, the Body and Blood of the Lord that will give you life. "I have come that they may have life, and have it to the full" (Jn 10:10). As manna nourished the Israelites on their journey to the Promised Land, so the Eucharist will nourish you on your road of hope (cf. Jn 6:50).

6   Wear one garment and speak one language: charity. Charity is the sign that you are a disciple of the Lord (cf. Jn 13:35). It is the least expensive brand-name, but the hardest to find. Charity is the principle "language." Saint Paul considered it more precious than "speaking the languages of men and angels" (cf. 1 Cor 13:1). It will be the only language in heaven.

7   Hold firmly to one guiding principle: prayer. No one is stronger than the person who prays because the Lord has promised to grant everything to those who pray. When you are united in prayer the Lord is present among you (cf. Mt 18:20). I recommend this to you with all my heart: in addition to times of communal prayer, withdraw every day for an hour, or even better for two if you can, for personal prayer. I assure you that it will not be wasted time! In my experience over all these years, I have seen confirmed the words of Saint Teresa of Avila: "Whoever does not pray does not need the devil to lead him off the path: he will throw himself into hell."

8   Observe one rule: the Gospel. This "constitution" is superior to all others. It is the constitution that Jesus left his apostles (cf. Mt 4:23). It is not

difficult, complicated, or legalistic like others. On the contrary, it is dynamic, gentle, and stimulating for your soul. A saint separated from the Gospel is a false saint!

9 Loyally follow one leader: Jesus Christ, and his representatives on earth: the Holy Father and the bishops, successors of the Apostles (cf. Jn 20:22–23). Live and die for the Church as Christ did. Do not forget, however, that living for the Church entail as much sacrifice as dying for the Church.

10 Cultivate a special love for Mary. Saint John Mary Vianney used to confide: "After Jesus, my first love is Mary." If you listen to Mary you will not lose your way. Whatever you undertake in her name will not fail. Honor her and you will gain eternal life.

11 Take as your one wisdom the science of the Cross (cf. 1 Cor 2:2). Look to the Cross and you will find the solution to all the problems that assail you. If the Cross is your criterion for making choices and decisions, you will be at peace.

12 Have one ideal: to turn toward God the Father, a Father who is all love. The whole of our Lord's life, his every thought and deed, had but one goal:

"the world must know that I love the Father, just as the Father has commanded me, that is what I will do" (Jn 14:3 1), and "I always do what is pleasing to him" (Jn 8:29).

13 There is only one thing you must fear: sin. When the court of the Greek emperor held a meeting to discuss the question of how to take revenge on Saint John Chrysostom for his forthright denunciation of the empress, the following plans were suggested:

a) Cast him into prison. "But there he will have the opportunity to pray and suffer for the Lord as he has always desired."

b) Banishment. "But, for him, everywhere is the Lord's country."

c) The death penalty. "But, thus he will be a martyr and we will satisfy his aspirations to go to the Lord. None of these plans will cause him to suffer; on the contrary, he will joyfully accept them."

d) "There is only one thing of which he hates above all else—sin; but it would be impossible to force him to commit sin!"

Therefore, if your only fear is sin, no one will be stronger than you.

14 Cherish one desire: "Thy kingdom come; Thy will be done on earth as it is in heaven" (Mt 6:10), so that throughout the earth all nations will know God as he is known in heaven; so that on this earth everyone will begin to love one another as in heaven; so that also on this earth there will be the beatitude that there is in heaven. Make the effort to spread this desire. Begin now to bring the happiness of heaven to everyone in this world.

15 There is only one thing lacking: "Go home and sell all that belongs to you; give it to the poor, and so the treasure you have shall be in heaven; then come back and follow me" (Mk 10:21). You have to make up your mind once and for all. Our Lord wants volunteers free from other attachments.

16 For your apostolate use the one most effective means: personal contact. With this you enter into the lives of others, you understand them and love them. Personal relationships are more effective than preaching and writing books. Contact between people and "heart to heart" exchanges will be the secret of your perseverance and your success.

17 There is only one truly important thing: "Mary chose the better part" when she sat at the Lord's

feet (Lk 10:41–42). If you are not living an interior life, If Jesus is not the very life and soul of
your activities then. . . . You fully understand the
consequences of such living and so there is no
need for me to repeat them here.

18 Your only food: "The Father's will" (Jn 4:34));
    that is, you live and grow by the will of God. Your
    actions proceed from the will of God. The will of
    God is like food which makes you live strongly
    and happily; if you live apart from the will of God,
    you will die.

19 You have only one moment which is the most
    beautiful: the present moment (cf. Mt 6:34, Jas
    4:13–15). Live it completely in the love of God.
    If your life is built up like a large crystal from
    millions of such beautiful moments, it will be a
    wonderfully beautiful life. Do you see how easy
    it is?

20 Have one "magna carta": the Beatitudes (Mt
    5:3–12). Jesus proclaimed them in the Sermon
    on the Mount. Live according to them and you
    will experience a happiness which you will then
    communicate to all whom you meet.

21 Have only one important objective: your duty. It is
    not important if it is large or small, because when

you do your duty you are collaborating with the Heavenly Father, who has determined that this is the work that you alone must do to carry out his plan in history (cf. Lk 2:49, Jn 17:4). Many people invent complicated ways of practicing virtue and then they complain how difficult it is, but doing your duty is the most certain and simplest path of virtue you can follow.

22   Have one way of becoming holy: the grace of God and your will to live by grace (cf. 1 Cor 15:10). God will never be lacking with his grace; but is your will strong enough?

23   You have only one reward: God himself. When God asked Saint Thomas Aquinas: "You have written well of me, Thomas; what reward do you desire?" Saint Thomas replied, "Only you, Lord."

24   ...You have one homeland,
the bell rings, grave, deep,

Vietnam prays.
The bell rings still, sharp, charged with
      emotion,
Vietnam weeps.
The bell rings again, vibrant, pathetic,
Vietnam triumphs.

The bell tolls, crystalline
Vietnam hopes.

You have one homeland, Vietnam;
a country so beloved, through the centuries.
It is your pride, your joy.
Love her mountains and her rivers,
her brocade and satin landscapes,
her glorious history,
her hard-working people,
her heroic defenders.

The raging rivers run
as does the blood of her people.
Her mountains are high,
but higher still the bones that are piled there.
The land is narrow, but her ambition vast,
O little country much renowned!

Help your homeland with your whole self,
be faithful to her,
defend her with your body and blood,
build her up with your heart and mind,
share the joy of your brothers and sisters,
and the sadness of your people.

One Vietnam.
One people.

One soul.
One culture.
One tradition.

Catholics of Vietnam,
love a thousand times your homeland!
The Lord teaches you, the Church asks you—
may the love of your country be fully one
with the blood that runs through your veins.

House arrest in forced residence
Cây Vông (Nha Trang, Central Vietnam)
December 8, 1975, Solemnity of Immaculate Conception

My Choice Is Jesus

Lord Jesus, on the path of hope
two thousand years long,
your love, like a wave,
has lifted many pilgrims.
You have loved with an aching love
their thoughts, their words, their actions.
You have loved them with a heart
stronger than temptation, stronger than
    suffering,
stronger even than death.
They have been your word in the world.
Their lives have been a revolution
that has renewed the face of the Church.

Contemplating from childhood
these shining examples,
I conceived a dream:
to offer you my whole life,
the only life I have to live,
for an eternal and unalterable ideal.
I have decided!
If I fulfill your will
you will achieve this ideal in me,
and I will throw myself into this wonderful
    adventure.

I have chosen you,

I have no regrets.

I hear you say to me:

"Remain in me. Remain in my love!"

But how can I remain in another?

Only love can achieve this extraordinary
mystery.

I understand that you want my whole life.

"Everything! And for your love!"

On the path of hope I follow your every step:

1   Your wandering steps toward the stable in
Bethlehem.

2   Your worried steps on the road to Egypt.

3   Your rapid steps to the house of Nazareth.

4   Your joyful steps on the way to the Temple
with your parents.

5   Your weary steps during thirty years of work.

6   Your solicitous steps in your three years of
preaching the Good News.

7   Your hurried steps to seek out the lost sheep.

8   Your sorrowful steps on entering Jerusalem.

9   Your solitary steps before the Praetorium.

10 Your steps weighed down by the Cross on
the road to Calvary.

11   Your failed steps, dead and buried in a
tomb not your own.
Stripped of everything,
without clothes, without a friend,
abandoned even by your Father,
you were always submissive to your Father.
Lord Jesus, on my knees,
turning toward you, being for you,
in front of the tabernacle,
I understand:
I could not choose any other road,
any happier road,
even if by appearances
another road seemed more glorious,
for you, eternal friend,
the only friend of my life,
would not be present there.
In you with the Trinity is all of heaven,
the whole world, and all humanity.
Your sufferings are mine.
The sufferings of humanity are mine.
Mine are all things, where there is no peace
        or joy,
or beauty, or comfort, or friendliness.
Mine are all sadness, delusions,
divisions, abandonment, disgrace.

Let whatever is yours come to me
because you have born it all.
Let whatever is in my brothers and sisters
    come to me,
because you are in them.
I firmly believe in you,

12   because you have taken the steps of triumph:
"Take courage; I have conquered the world!"
(Jn 16:34)

13   You have told me: walk with giant steps,
go all over the world,
proclaim the Good News,
dry tears of sorrow,
reassure discouraged hearts,
reunite divided hearts,
embrace the world with the ardor of your love,
do away with what must be eradicated,
leave only truth, justice, love.
But Lord, I know my weaknesses!
Free me from egoism, from defenses,
so that I no longer fear the suffering,
which torments—
unworthy of an apostle.
Render me strong for this adventure.
Help me not to worry about the world's
    wisdom.

I accept being treated as someone who is crazy
for Jesus, Mary, and Joseph . . .
I want to put myself to the test,
to be ready for every circumstance,
heedless of the consequences,
because you have taught me
to confront every event.
If you send me to the Cross
I will let myself be crucified.
If you send me into the silence
of your tabernacle even until the end of time,

14   I will enter therein with daring steps.
I will lose everything, but I will stay with
      you.
Your love will be there
to flood my heart with love for all.
My happiness will be complete . . .
It is for this reason that I repeat: I have
      chosen you.
I want nothing save you and your glory.

House arrest in forced residence,
Giang Xá (North Vietnam)
March 19, 1980, Solemnity of Saint Joseph,
husband of Mary

Are you inspired by the words of Cardinal Văn Thuận after reading this small book? Then don't miss reading his biography, *The Miracle of Hope*. Find out the secrets of his spirituality that sustained him during his long dark night of imprisonment. Written by André Van Chau, a close friend of Văn Thuận, *The Miracle of Hope* reveals the heart of this great hero of our times. He continued to proclaim the gospel of peace and freedom, justice and human dignity until his death in 2002. Destined to become contemporary classics, Van Thuan's writings have inspired hope in millions.

0-8198-4822-0
$12.95

BOOKS & MEDIA

A mission of the Daughters of St. Paul

As apostles of Jesus Christ, evangelizing today's world:

We are CALLED to holiness
by God's living Word and Eucharist.

We COMMUNICATE the Gospel message
through our lives and through all
available forms of media.

We SERVE the Church
by responding to the hopes and needs
of all people with the Word of God,
in the spirit of St. Paul.

For more information visit us at
www.pauline.org.

BOOKS & MEDIA

The Daughters of St. Paul operate book and media centers at the following addresses. Visit, call, or write the one nearest you today, or find us at www.paulinestore.org.

CALIFORNIA
3908 Sepulveda Blvd, Culver City, CA 90230   310-397-8676
3250 Middlefield Road, Menlo Park, CA 94025   650-562-7060

FLORIDA
145 S.W. 107th Avenue, Miami, FL 33174   305-559-6715

HAWAII
1143 Bishop Street, Honolulu, HI 96813   808-521-2731

ILLINOIS
172 North Michigan Avenue, Chicago, IL 60601   312-346-4228

LOUISIANA
4403 Veterans Memorial Blvd, Metairie, LA 70006   504-887-7631

MASSACHUSETTS
885 Providence Hwy, Dedham, MA 02026   781-326-5385

MISSOURI
9804 Watson Road, St. Louis, MO 63126   314-965-3512

NEW YORK
115 E. 29th Street, New York City, NY 10016   212-754-1110

SOUTH CAROLINA
243 King Street, Charleston, SC 29401   843-577-0175

TEXAS
No book center; for parish exhibits or outreach evangelization, contact: 210-569-0500, or SanAntonio@paulinemedia.com, or P.O. Box 761416, San Antonio, TX 78245

VIRGINIA
1025 King Street, Alexandria, VA 22314   703-549-3806

CANADA
3022 Dufferin Street, Toronto, ON M6B 3T5   416-781-9131